HORIZONS plus
SCIENCE
Stories

Silver Burdett & Ginn
MORRISTOWN, NJ ▪ NEEDHAM, MA
Atlanta, GA ▪ Cincinnati, OH ▪ Dallas, TX ▪ Deerfield, IL ▪ Menlo Park, CA

D1276136

This product was created by the Horizons Plus staff at the Houston Museum of Natural Science for final production by Silver Burdett & Ginn.

This material is based upon work supported by the National Science Foundation. Any opinions, findings, conclusions, or recommendations expressed in this particular publication are those of the authors and do not necessarily reflect the views of the National Science Foundation or the Houston Museum of Natural Science.

ISBN 0-382-17501-8

Table of Contents

Galapagos

by Gary Young and Carolyn Sumners · illustrated by Mark Bellerose

Hans had never felt so hot. Yet Maria laughed as she ran across a dusty street in Puerto Ayora. "How can she run in this weather?" Hans thought. His friends back home in Norway would never believe it could get this hot.

Hans was spending the summer with his Uncle Kurt in the Galapagos Islands. Uncle Kurt had asked Maria, the daughter of an old friend, to show Hans the giant tortoises of Santa Cruz Island.

Carefully Hans followed Maria over a rocky ridge. Maria pointed to a pool filled with large, bumpy boulders. Suddenly one of the boulders moved and a head peeked out. Then the "boulder" sprouted legs and stood up. It was the biggest tortoise Hans had ever seen.

"Wow!" he exclaimed. "It's huge!"

Maria nodded. "Our islands were named for these tortoises. Galapagos means tortoises in Spanish."

"Do tortoises like these live on every island?" asked Hans.

Maria shook her head. "No. Many have died off. There are still giant tortoises on a couple of the other islands," she added, "but they're not exactly like these. Here the tortoises have dome-shaped shells that fit close to their bodies. Other tortoises have shells that look like saddles. Those tortoises have longer necks, too."

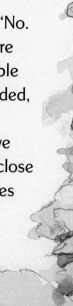

"You'd think they'd be the same on all islands," Hans said.

"Oh, no," said Maria. "Islands like Española and Pinta are different from Santa Cruz, even though they're all part of the Galapagos. For example, here there are lots of plants for tortoises to eat. Española has just cactus and spiny bushes. Long ago Española had many tortoises. They quickly ate the parts of the cactus that were easy to reach.

"Tortoises with longer necks and legs could eat parts that grew higher on the cactus. The saddle-shaped shells allowed them to reach even more food. In time, only the tortoises with longer necks, longer legs, and "saddleback" shells survived on Española. They were adapted to their environment."

Hans watched a tiny bird land on the neck of the biggest tortoise. "Look," Hans shouted, "a little bird is attacking a tortoise."

Maria laughed. "No he's not, and Big Juan doesn't mind," she said. "Big Juan's the oldest tortoise on the island, and that finch is doing him a favor."

Hans couldn't imagine how the finch could be helping the big reptile.

Maria laughed at Hans's expression. "The finch is eating ticks on Big Juan's skin. Finches are adapted to the islands, too. Some have big, heavy bills for eating seeds; some have pointed bills for eating insects in trees. We have about thirteen different kinds."

"Well," replied Hans, "I bet Big Juan wouldn't mind if we scared off the finch."

"No," said Maria, "that wouldn't be right. Here we let animals live naturally. People don't interfere with wildlife."

That evening at dinner, Hans told his uncle about the day's adventures. Uncle Kurt roared with laughter as Hans described his meeting with Big Juan.

"Yes," Uncle Kurt smiled fondly, "I remember meeting Big Juan the first time I visited here. In fact, it was Maria's father who introduced me to him, long before Maria was born. Tortoises can live for more than a hundred years."

"The Galapagos Islands are special, aren't they?" Hans asked.

"They're special for many reasons," Uncle Kurt agreed. "You're just beginning to discover some of those reasons."

"Well," said Hans, "I know they're special because people aren't allowed to interfere with animals." Uncle Kurt nodded. "I bet comparing the same animals from different islands helps us see how animal and plant life develops," Hans continued.

"That's right," said Uncle Kurt, "there are many kinds of animals to study: reptiles like Big Juan, birds, and . . . " Uncle Kurt noticed that Hans had stopped smiling. "What's the matter?" he asked.

"Nothing, really, Uncle Kurt," he replied slowly. "It's just that the heat really gets to me, but it doesn't seem to bother Maria at all."

"Just wait, Hans," Uncle Kurt said. "You will get used to the heat. Think of the tortoises and birds who had to adapt to each particular island."

"That took thousands of years," Hans grumbled.

Uncle Kurt laughed. "Adaptations do take thousands of years,

but getting used to a place can happen much more quickly."

The next afternoon Hans and Maria explored San Cristobal Island. "Look," Maria called. "A frigatebird." Hans looked up at a beautiful black bird with a two-meter wing span and a long, forked tail.

"Watch it steal fish from that booby." Maria pointed to a bird eating a fish near the surf.

"Is this what they call a 'booby trap'?" Hans grinned. Maria rolled her eyes. The frigatebird suddenly soared down once and then again, just in time to catch the fish the startled booby had dropped.

"I feel sorry for the booby," Hans said. "The frigatebird doesn't get all the food." Maria walked right up to the booby. Hans was amazed the bird didn't fly away.

"It's a red-footed booby," Maria said. "It can grasp tree limbs with its feet, unlike the blue-footed booby. It seems very curious about you," Maria giggled.

"I feel strange," Hans sighed. "I'm not used to such a warm climate."

"I was just kidding," she smiled, "but let's ask your uncle to take us to Bolivar Channel. I can show you a bird that seems more out of place than you do."

When Uncle Kurt heard what Maria had said to Hans, he laughed and agreed to take them to Bolivar Channel the next day.

"What's so funny?" Hans wondered.

The following morning Uncle Kurt, Hans, and Maria climbed into a motorboat to visit the birds that reminded Maria of Hans. It was a warm day, and the water looked inviting from the boat. Hans asked if there was a spot where they could stop and swim.

"Not near here," Uncle Kurt replied. "The water is very cold. An ocean current from Antarctica comes right through here."

Hans looked at the water and sighed. Then he heard Uncle Kurt and Maria giggling.

"What's so funny?" asked Hans. The two laughed even harder.

Uncle Kurt rounded the south end of Isabella Island, and Maria looked at Hans with laughing eyes. "So, Hans, do you still feel like you don't belong here?" Hans looked over towards shore. "See, Hans," Maria shouted. She was pointing to some penguins splashing along the shoreline.

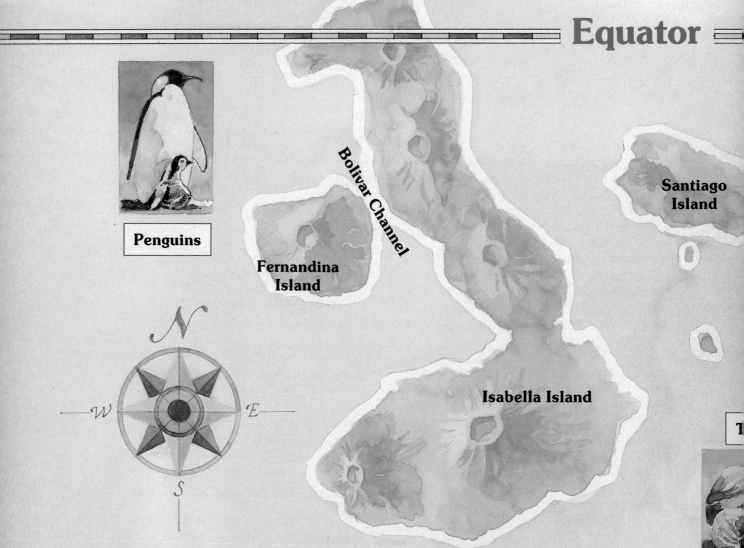

Equator

Penguins

Bolivar Channel

Fernandina Island

Isabella Island

Santiago Island

N
W E
S

"Penguins near the equator?" Hans exclaimed. He was really surprised. "How did they adapt to this warm climate?" He remembered that the islands are in the path of a cold ocean current. "Well, if penguins can live here, I can stop complaining," he said. Uncle Kurt winked.

Then Maria clapped her hands and said, "I've got a great idea! I know the perfect place for Hans to go swimming." She cupped her hand and whispered something in Uncle Kurt's ear.

"Yes, indeed," Uncle Kurt said, "that is a great idea."

"This is my favorite place to go swimming," Maria told Hans. "I think you're going to like it."

Uncle Kurt guided the boat back towards Santa Cruz. Then he headed towards Eden Island. Hans was excited. So far, everything Maria had shown him had been different and interesting.

Sea Lion

Partial Map of Galapagos Islands

Eden Island

Santa Cruz Island

San Cristobal Island

Frigatebird

Floreana Island

Española Island

Uncle Kurt anchored the boat a short distance from shore in a protected cove. Hans looked around. "Yes," he thought, "this is a special place." He grinned at Maria and his uncle and said, "You're right, this is a great place to go swimming."

Uncle Kurt slipped into the water first and then helped Maria and Hans in. Hans swam around happily, and he turned to tell Maria how good it felt. Instead, he found he was swimming with a sea lion! The sea lion splashed and swam just a few feet from Hans as if they were old friends. Maria said that sea lions enjoy sharing the ocean with people, but they don't like to be touched. Hans remembered that people weren't supposed to interfere with the wildlife on the islands.

Soon the three people swam to shore. Hans was tired but happy as he pulled himself onto a rock next to his uncle. He noticed that even Maria seemed tired. "You know," said Hans, "if the penguins remind you of me, the sea lions remind me of you."

"Why?" asked Maria.

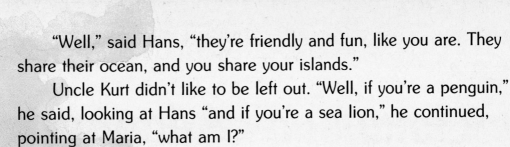

"Well," said Hans, "they're friendly and fun, like you are. They share their ocean, and you share your islands."

Uncle Kurt didn't like to be left out. "Well, if you're a penguin," he said, looking at Hans "and if you're a sea lion," he continued, pointing at Maria, "what am I?"

"Big Juan!" Hans and Maria cried.

Uncle Kurt frowned. "Be fair. I'm not *that* old!"

Hans felt happy. He would get used to the islands after all. He knew that when he returned to Norway, he would tell his friends how he walked with wild birds and swam with sea lions. The summer wasn't over — he would have lots more to tell them before he left these wonderful islands.

◈ **Reader's Response**
What would you enjoy most about visiting the Galapagos Islands?

Galapagos Adaptations

In the 1800s Charles Darwin visited the Galapagos Islands. He was interested in the animals he saw there, especially the finches. Why did one group of birds have so many different kinds of beaks? Thinking about finches and other animals eventually led to his famous theory of evolution, which explains that animals adapt to their environments.

The chart shows some of the finches found in the Galapagos. Notice the different bills and the purpose each one serves.

Warbler Finch	**Vegetarian Finch**	**Large Ground Finch**	**Small Cactus Finch**	**Woodpecker Finch**
These birds have slim bills adapted for eating insects.	It lives in humid highlands and is presumed to eat fruit, soft seeds, and insects.	The bill of this bird has developed into a good seed crusher, so this finch can eat seeds on the ground.	This bird spends most of its time in trees or cacti. The black bill means that it is ready to breed.	This bird can hold twigs to pry insect larvae out of small holes or from under tree bark.

Compare the first and third finches. How are they alike and how are they different?

Problem Solving

Choose an animal, think about how it looks, and tell what kind of adaptation to its environment it has and why. You may want to choose an animal from the list below.

frog	woodpecker	polar bear	squirrel	seal	porcupine
clam	hummingbird	octopus	giraffe	whale	anteater

Show What You Know

1. Tell about two birds that live on the Galapagos Islands.
2. How have adaptations helped the animals in the story?
3. Why are scientists interested in the Galapagos Islands?

Creative Writing

A travel agency has hired you to write an article for tourists entitled "The Amazing Galapagos Islands." In the first paragraph, explain what tourists might find interesting about the islands. In the second paragraph, point out what rules tourists should follow for the sake of the animals. In the last paragraph, tell what the weather is like and what clothes might be needed.

PHOTOSYNTHESIS CALLS IT QUITS!

by
Grace H. Boyle

illustrated by
Joseph Veno

Johnnie Arnold sat at his desk with his science book open in front of him. He knew he shouldn't have waited until the night before the test to study, and he knew he shouldn't have waited until after baseball practice. He was so tired now. He also knew he shouldn't have watched that horror movie on television after dinner. He knew a lot, but unfortunately not very much of it had to do with photosynthesis.

Johnnie looked down at his book again. "Photosynthesis is the process by which green plants use light, water, and carbon dioxide to make food. The green chlorophyll in plants traps light energy from the sun. This light energy is used to change water and carbon dioxide into sugar and oxygen," Johnnie read. The print on the page began to blur. Johnnie's eyes began to close. His head began to droop. "Photosynthesis . . . photosynthesis . . . photosynthesis . . ." Johnnie drifted off to sleep.

Suddenly he found himself walking down a street in a town that looked a lot like his town. But everything seemed foggy. There were no people around. It was quiet — too quiet.

Johnnie came to a corner and saw a newspaper vending machine. The headline of the paper screamed, "PHOTOSYNTHESIS CALLS IT QUITS!" Johnnie bent down to get a closer look at the newspaper. The article continued.

"Scientists gathered today to discuss the sudden breakdown of the photosynthesis process. The world has been reeling from the effects of the (continued on page 10)"

Johnnie looked around. Where were all the people? Where were the cars and trucks that usually made his mom complain about all the noise? He walked past Ruby's Department Store. This morning the front window had been full of sweaters. Now it was completely empty! He continued past the drugstore. Its windows were almost empty, too!

Did all this have something to do with photosynthesis breaking down? Photosynthesis! Photosynthesis! Johnnie tried to remember what Mrs. Grayson, his teacher, had said about photosynthesis and the importance of plants. When Mrs. Grayson had asked the class to imagine a world without green plants, he had thought it didn't sound so bad. No green plants would mean no broccoli, no spinach, and best of all, no grass to mow.

BUTCHER SHOP

CHOICE MEATS A

PHOTOSYNTHESIS CALLS IT QUITS!

DAILY PLANET

DAILY PLANET

21

Soon, Johnnie came to Mr. Jessup's butcher shop. Usually it was full of chickens, steaks, roasts, and chops. Johnnie looked through the window. The cases and counters were empty. Mr. Jessup was sitting by the counter resting his head on his hands.

"Mr. Jessup!" Johnnie yelled, running into the store. "Where is everyone? Why are all the stores empty? What's wrong?"

Mr. Jessup looked up. "What's wrong, Johnnie? No photosynthesis, that's what's wrong. No photosynthesis — no lamb chops." The unhappy butcher pointed sadly at his empty counters and cases. Then he disappeared into the mist.

"Mr. Jessup! Wait!" Johnnie yelled, but the man was gone.

Johnnie wandered back out to the sidewalk. He knew that no photosynthesis meant no green plants—but no lamb chops? Johnnie walked on to the park. At least, it used to be a park. Now, with photosynthesis calling it quits, there were no flowers and no trees, no green plants, and no grass.

Johnnie noticed the hill where he sledded in the winter. It was cut by huge gullies where rain had washed away the soil. Johnnie sat down on a rock. He realized that the roots of plants and trees had held the soil in place. With the green plants gone, all the soil was washing away. He had to do something about getting photosynthesis working again, and soon!

The world needed the grass to help keep soil from eroding. And Johnnie realized the world needed grass and other plants for sheep to eat so that there would be lamb chops for food and wool for clothing. That's why the butcher shop and the department store windows were empty. And Johnnie remembered that lots of medicines come from plants, and that's why the drugstore was almost empty.

So much depended on plants and photosynthesis. Hadn't he read that during photosynthesis, plants release oxygen that people need to breathe? Photosynthesis was more important than he had ever imagined.

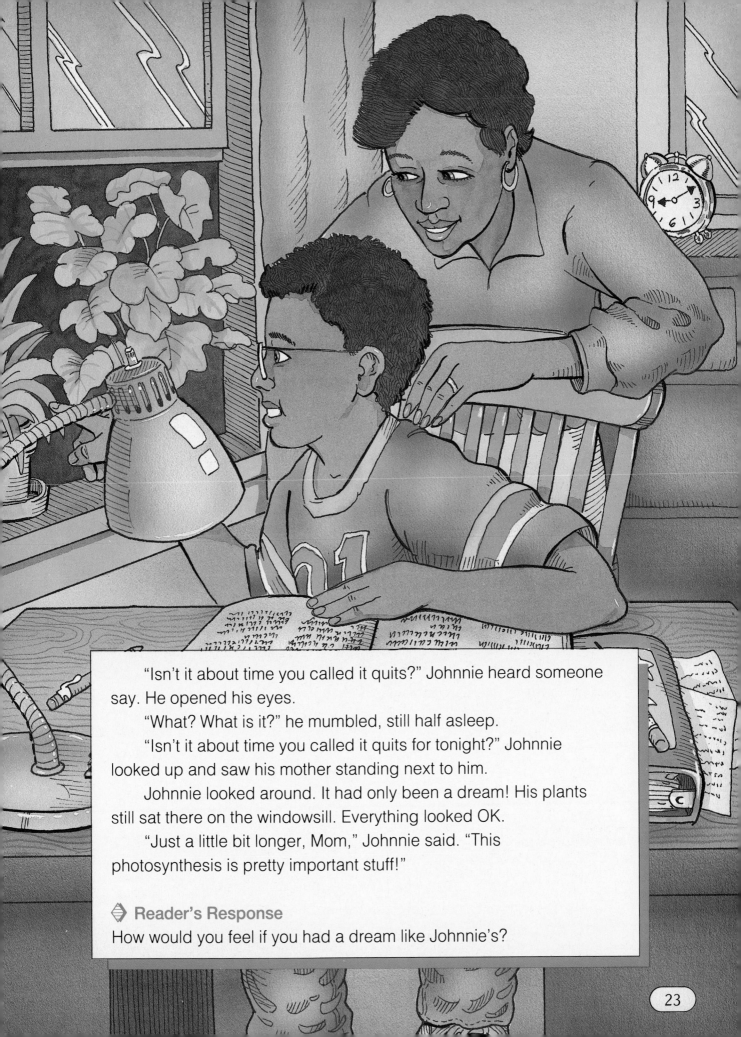

"Isn't it about time you called it quits?" Johnnie heard someone say. He opened his eyes.

"What? What is it?" he mumbled, still half asleep.

"Isn't it about time you called it quits for tonight?" Johnnie looked up and saw his mother standing next to him.

Johnnie looked around. It had only been a dream! His plants still sat there on the windowsill. Everything looked OK.

"Just a little bit longer, Mom," Johnnie said. "This photosynthesis is pretty important stuff!"

◆ Reader's Response

How would you feel if you had a dream like Johnnie's?

PLANTS

Plants release oxygen into the air and provide us with many of the things we use in our lives.

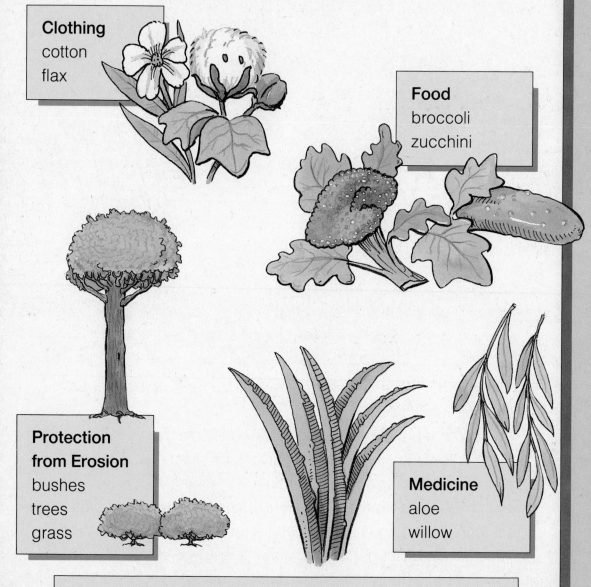

Clothing
cotton
flax

Food
broccoli
zucchini

Protection from Erosion
bushes
trees
grass

Medicine
aloe
willow

Think of other ways in which we depend upon plants. Name some other plants we use either directly or indirectly.

Problem Solving

In Johnnie's dream, a breakdown in the photosynthesis process causes troubles for green plants and people. In real life, plants are threatened by other problems, such as drought, over-cutting, and pollution. Can you think of some possible solutions to these problems?

Show What You Know

1. What is photosynthesis?
2. What do plants release during photosynthesis?
3. Name one way plants are important to people.

Creative Writing

Imagine the world was missing just one plant — for example, a world without grass, or apple trees, or cotton plants. Think about the effect this might have, and write a paragraph about life without this plant.

The Ospreys of Great Island

by Christie Hoagland
illustrated by
Byrna Waldman

"Look!" exclaimed Erika. "There's an osprey, just like the ones we have back home in Maine." Erika was spending the summer with her grandparents on the coast of Connecticut.

"That's a sight for sore eyes," Gramps said, looking at the bird's white underbelly and the band of dark brown feathers on its head. "We don't see one of those very often."

"Why not?" asked Erika. "I thought ospreys liked to live near the ocean."

"They do. We used to have lots of them around here," her grandmother said.

"Where did they all go?" asked Erika.

"Many things have changed," her grandmother replied, "and the changes have made it harder for ospreys to live here. I can explain it if you'd like."

"Oh, that's okay," said Erika. She didn't think change could be blamed for everything, and she liked lots of things about the present. She decided to find out for herself why the ospreys left.

The next morning, Erika pulled her bike out of the garage and pedaled to the public library. There she learned that ospreys live in tall trees where animals such as raccoons cannot steal their eggs. She also learned that they eat fish. The books contained many facts — except why ospreys had left the area.

If Erika had asked the librarian, she would have found the answer in newspaper and magazine articles — but she didn't.

After she left the library, Erika went to the hardware store and talked to the owner, Pete Fry. Pete was one of the oldest residents in town, but it turned out he wasn't much interested in birds. He hadn't really noticed the missing ospreys.

If Erika had talked to Pete's wife behind the cash register, she would have found out what she wanted to know — but she didn't.

When Erika got home, she saw Betsy, a college student who lived next door, sitting on her porch. Erika walked up, said "Hi," sat down, and put her head in her hands.

"What's wrong?" asked Betsy.

"I saw an osprey," Erika answered.

"Really? Why, that's wonderful," she said. "You should feel happy. There aren't many around anymore."

"I know," Erika moaned, "but why?"

"Ask your grandparents," she replied.

"My grandparents!"

"Yes," she smiled. "They know quite a lot about why the osprey population decreased."

"They just say that things used to be better," Erika sighed.

"Life was better for the ospreys many years ago," Betsy said. "But the osprey population decreased tremendously when my father was young, so there weren't many around even when I was growing up. I think you'll find that your grandparents have a lot to tell you. Come on, I'll go with you."

"Betsy said you can explain about the ospreys," Erika said when she and Betsy joined her grandparents in the living room. "Why did they go away?"

"They didn't just 'go away,'" said Gramps. "Their population decreased because fewer were born and fewer were able to survive."

"Show Erika some of the pictures from your photo album," suggested Betsy. "Maybe that will help her to understand."

Grandma opened the album and pointed to a photograph. It was an old picture of young people. They were standing together in an open field. Far in the background Erika could see a marsh and ocean. On the left stood lots of trees and bushes.

"That's your grandfather," said Grandma, pointing to a young man about twenty years old, "and that's me," she added, pointing to a girl with a sunny smile. "That's Betsy's father over there," she said. "He's the little fellow holding onto Gramps's hand." Erika's eyes widened. It was hard to think of these young people as her grandparents.

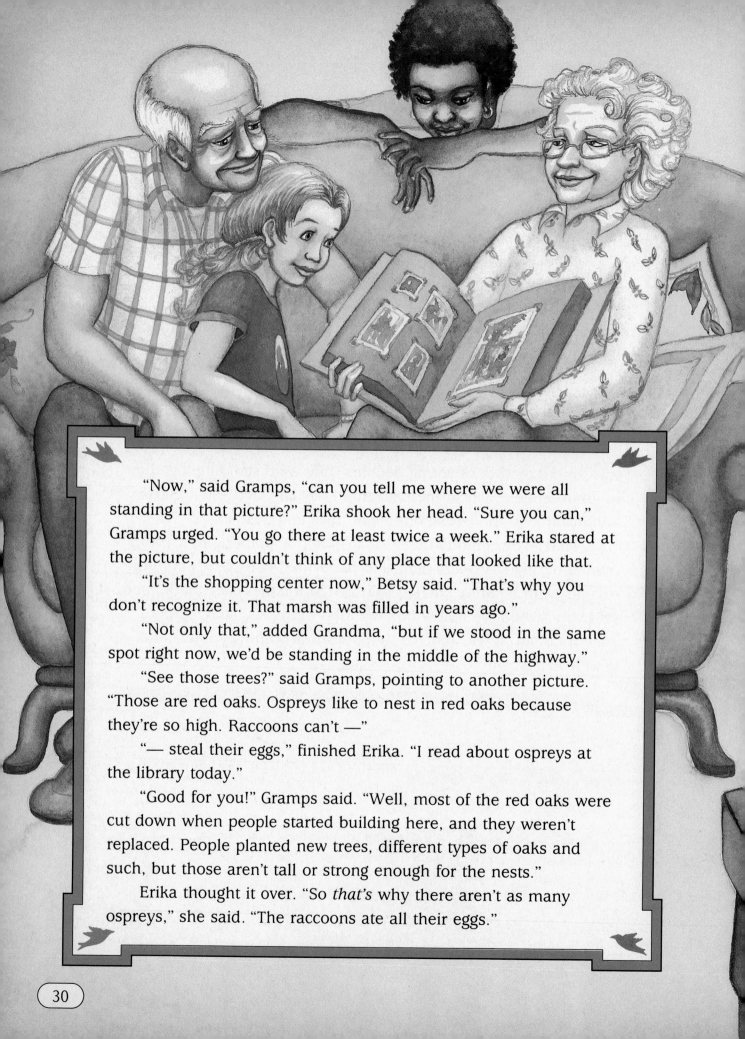

"Now," said Gramps, "can you tell me where we were all standing in that picture?" Erika shook her head. "Sure you can," Gramps urged. "You go there at least twice a week." Erika stared at the picture, but couldn't think of any place that looked like that.

"It's the shopping center now," Betsy said. "That's why you don't recognize it. That marsh was filled in years ago."

"Not only that," added Grandma, "but if we stood in the same spot right now, we'd be standing in the middle of the highway."

"See those trees?" said Gramps, pointing to another picture. "Those are red oaks. Ospreys like to nest in red oaks because they're so high. Raccoons can't —"

"— steal their eggs," finished Erika. "I read about ospreys at the library today."

"Good for you!" Gramps said. "Well, most of the red oaks were cut down when people started building here, and they weren't replaced. People planted new trees, different types of oaks and such, but those aren't tall or strong enough for the nests."

Erika thought it over. "So *that's* why there aren't as many ospreys," she said. "The raccoons ate all their eggs."

"Well," said Grandma, "there were other changes, too."

"That's right," said Betsy, nodding her head. "Ospreys are part of an ecosystem. An ecosystem is a place where living and nonliving things affect each other. Within the ospreys' ecosystem, their food supply became polluted.

"Several years ago," Betsy continued, "your grandparents had been counting the eggs in the few osprey nests left, when they noticed something strange. Many of the eggs were broken."

Grandma nodded. "When we examined the eggs closely, we saw that the shells were very thin. The shells broke as soon as the eggs were laid."

"So," said Betsy, "your grandparents had the eggshells tested. They learned that the shells had been affected by DDT, an insect poison that had gotten into the ospreys' food supply."

"Where did you find the eggs?" asked Erika.

"On Great Island," said Grandma, "where there are still a few ospreys left. And if they're left alone, maybe more will survive."

"Haven't you told Erika what you've done?" asked Betsy.

Gramps and Grandma shook their heads.

"Well," Betsy said, turning to Erika, "you're in for a treat. Do you want to take a canoe out to Great Island with me tomorrow?"

"Sure," Erika replied.

The next day on their way to Great Island, Betsy explained to Erika how the DDT got into ospreys' eggs.

"When DDT was used to kill insects, it was sprayed on the plants around here. It soaked into the soil, and then it drained into the water under the ground. This water, which was polluted with DDT, ran into the marsh. The tiny plankton in the marsh absorbed it. When fish ate the plankton, the DDT got into their bodies."

"Then the ospreys ate the fish," Erika said, "and the DDT ended up harming the ospreys' eggs."

Betsy nodded and then motioned to the shore. "We're almost there. Don't talk loudly. Noise frightens the wildlife."

Erika nodded. She didn't want to disturb the ospreys.

Betsy showed Erika what Gramps and Grandma had done. They had built platforms on very tall poles for the ospreys to nest in. This helped keep the osprey eggs safe from raccoons.

Betsy led Erika to a slope near the platforms. "From here," she whispered, "you might see an osprey sitting on her eggs."

Erika didn't see an osprey, but she was able to see two eggs in one of the nests! The eggs didn't seem to be broken.

Later Erika told her grandparents about the two eggs. They said that eggshells were stronger than they had been.

Erika was proud that her grandparents had worked to help ospreys. She didn't mind them talking about the past anymore. In fact, she began asking them about other things that had changed since they were young. Some of the changes were bad, thought Erika, but some were good, too.

She felt a little sad when she thought about the ospreys, though. "You know, Gramps," she said, "I hope the ospreys don't become extinct like the dinosaurs."

Erika's grandfather looked at her. "Not if we can help it," he said. Erika smiled. She decided then and there to help, too.

"If only I'd asked you about the ospreys in the first place," Erika sighed, "but I didn't."

◆ **Reader's Response**

What kinds of things from the past do you enjoy hearing about?

DDT in the Ecosystem

In "The Ospreys of Great Island," the word *population* means "the number of animals in an area." The population of ospreys in Connecticut refers to the total number of ospreys that live in that state.

Erika learns that one reason the population of ospreys in Connecticut declined was the use of DDT, an insect poison that got into their food. Below is a diagram that shows how DDT was carried into the ospreys' food and how it caused the population to decrease.

How did DDT get into the ecosystem?
How did the ospreys become affected by it?

Problem Solving

Animal populations often change over time. How could you find out if the animal populations in your community have increased or decreased?

Show What You Know

1. Where do ospreys like to live? What do they like to eat?

2. Name two changes that caused Connecticut's osprey population to decrease.

3. Explain how DDT got into the ospreys' food supply.

Creative Writing

At the end of the story Erika decides to help the ospreys survive. Pretend that you are Erika. Write a letter to your parents in Maine. Tell your parents how you plan to help the ospreys.

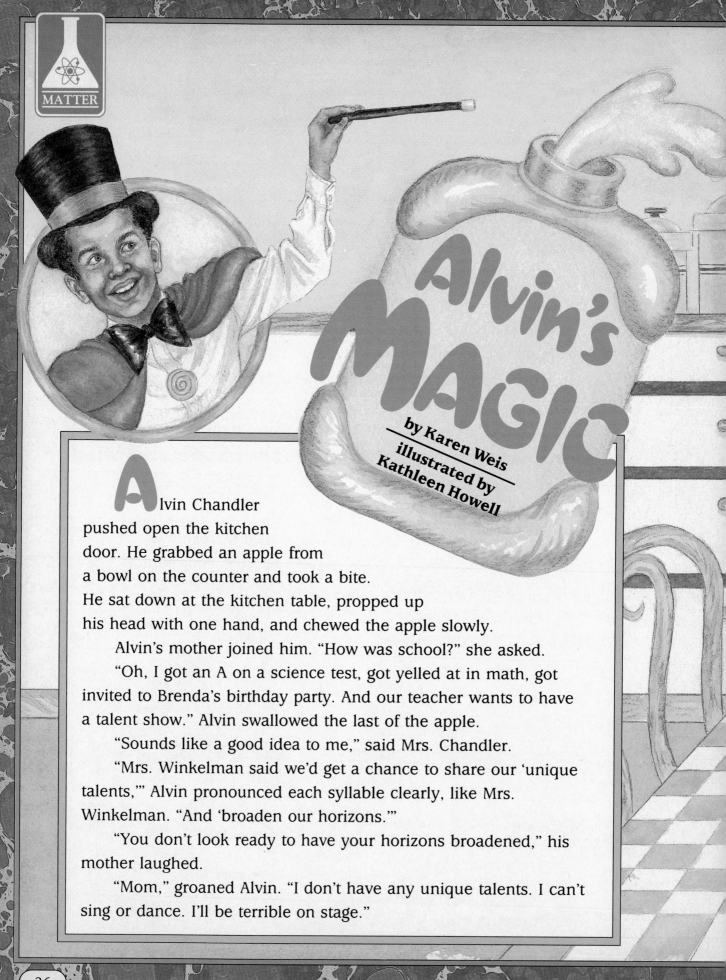

Alvin's MAGIC

by Karen Weis

illustrated by Kathleen Howell

Alvin Chandler pushed open the kitchen door. He grabbed an apple from a bowl on the counter and took a bite. He sat down at the kitchen table, propped up his head with one hand, and chewed the apple slowly.

Alvin's mother joined him. "How was school?" she asked.

"Oh, I got an A on a science test, got yelled at in math, got invited to Brenda's birthday party. And our teacher wants to have a talent show." Alvin swallowed the last of the apple.

"Sounds like a good idea to me," said Mrs. Chandler.

"Mrs. Winkelman said we'd get a chance to share our 'unique talents,'" Alvin pronounced each syllable clearly, like Mrs. Winkelman. "And 'broaden our horizons.'"

"You don't look ready to have your horizons broadened," his mother laughed.

"Mom," groaned Alvin. "I don't have any unique talents. I can't sing or dance. I'll be terrible on stage."

"That's not true. You're creative. You have lots of talents."

"Like what?" muttered Alvin.

"Like doing science experiments and building models. It takes talent and imagination to do that."

"Yeah, but that's not very entertaining. I can't build models in a talent show!" Alvin argued.

"Don't worry. I know you'll think of something."

All Alvin could do was imagine himself singing and dancing in front of the class while everyone laughed at him. It was a horrible thought!

At dinner Alvin picked at his food and stared down at the table. Where was his great imagination when he needed it? He fiddled with his fork and spoon. Then he played with the salt, pouring it into his glass of water until his father scolded him.

He stared at a bottle of salad dressing and read its label: "Aunt Angela's Real Oil and Vinegar Salad Dressing." When he shook the bottle, bubbles of oil floated through the vinegar. Alvin was surprised. He had never really looked at salad dressing before.

Then an idea struck him. "I'll do a magic show with liquids!"

"Mom," he said, "can I clean up the kitchen after dinner?"

"Alvin, you must be sick or in trouble. What have you done now?" asked his mother.

"I've had an idea. I know what to do for the talent show. But I need to work in the kitchen for a few hours."

"Alvin, what are you going to do?" his father asked.

"It's a surprise. I need to use a few clear bottles, some glasses, and a few other supplies," Alvin explained.

His mother was still unsure. "OK. But don't experiment with anything that could be dangerous, like soaps and cleaning fluids. And first you have to do the dinner dishes."

"That's a deal," Alvin replied.

Alvin washed the dishes and cleaned the kitchen counter. Then he collected the materials he would need. He took two eggs from the refrigerator. He gathered cooking oil, corn syrup, salt, and food colorings. He filled a pitcher with water. Then Alvin experimented for several hours.

Later that night, Mr. Chandler peeked into Alvin's kitchen lab. "Time to go to bed," he said.

Alvin quickly hid his experiment. "No problem, Dad. I've figured it all out."

"May I see?" Dad asked.

"No, Dad. You'll have to come to the talent show. It's going to be a surprise. May I borrow a few clear glasses?"

His father smiled. "Sure, Alvin. What will you call your act?"

Alvin thought for a moment. "How about 'Alvin's Magic'—the most mysterious act in the talent show!"

At last the night of the talent show arrived. Mrs. Winkelman's class had arranged their classroom like a little theater. The students had invited their parents to attend.

Some kids danced and sang. A few played musical instruments. One told silly jokes. Then came Alvin's turn. Wearing a red cape and carrying a long wand, Alvin rolled a small table onto the stage. A sign on the table said "Alvin the Magnificent." His classmates read the sign and laughed. Alvin just smiled.

Alvin raised two glasses of water and showed them to the audience. He placed an egg in the first glass, and it sank to the bottom. Then he waved his wand over the second glass, said "Alacazam!" and dropped another egg into the second glass.

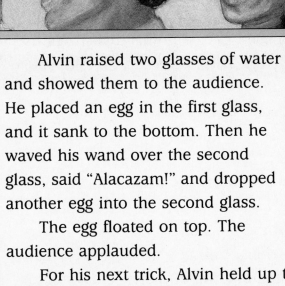

The egg floated on top. The audience applauded.

For his next trick, Alvin held up two bottles containing colored liquids. One was bright blue, the other yellow.

"What will happen," Alvin asked, "if I mix these two liquids?"

"They'll turn green," shouted one of Alvin's classmates.

"Absolutely correct!" said Alvin as he poured some blue liquid into the bottle of yellow liquid. The yellow liquid turned bright green. Then Alvin held up two more bottles. Again, one bottle contained blue liquid, the other yellow liquid.

"And if I mix these, what will happen?" asked Alvin.

"They'll turn green, too," said one person in the audience.

"That's what you think!" Alvin replied. He waved his magic wand over the bottles and shouted, "Alacazam! Alacazoo!"

Alvin opened the tops of the bottles. Very slowly he poured some of the yellow liquid into the bottle containing the blue liquid. He put the lid back on the bottle and shook it. The yellow liquid simply made waves in the blue liquid. Each color remained separate. The two colors never mixed.

The audience cheered. "Why don't they mix?" someone shouted.

"Well," Alvin answered, "it wasn't really because I said 'Alacazam'. The first two bottles contained water with food coloring. When I combined them, they mixed and formed green water. The second time, the blue liquid was water with blue food coloring, but the yellow liquid was oil. The oil floats on water."

"And why did the first egg sink and the second egg float in the water?" someone else asked.

"A magician isn't really supposed to explain his tricks," Alvin hesitated, "but since this is really science, not magic, I'll tell you. The two eggs are the same, but the liquids are different. The first glass has fresh water and the second has a salt water solution."

"Solution?" said Mary Lou, "Do you mean the answer to a problem?"

"No," said Alvin. "A solution also means a mixture formed by dissolving something in a liquid. I dissolved salt in water. That made the salt water heavier than the tap water."

"Very good," said Alvin's teacher. "I think it's also time to learn a new word: density. Density is the amount of matter packed into a given space. The density of the egg is greater than the density of tap water, so it drops to the bottom of the glass. The density of the egg is less than the density of salt water so the egg floats in salt water." Then she looked at the parents. "This year the students will study about density. Alvin has given us a good beginning."

"Wait, I've got one more trick!" Alvin held up the jar of blue and yellow liquids in one hand and a bottle containing an amber liquid in the other. Slowly he added the amber liquid to the yellow and blue liquids. The audience applauded as the amber liquid flowed down to the bottom of the jar. Alvin explained that the amber liquid was corn syrup, and that it was heavier than water. Then he smiled at his teacher. "Or, I should say that the density of the corn syrup is greater than the density of water."

Alvin winked as he rolled his magician's cart off stage. Two of the glasses clinked together. Alvin stopped for a second and listened to the sound. Off stage he clinked two other glasses together. "Next year I'll perform Alvin's Music," he thought.

◈ **Reader's Response**
If your class had a talent show, what would your act be?

DENSITY

Many of Alvin's "tricks" depended on the densities of different substances. Density is a property of all substances.

Small, heavy things like coins are very dense, while large, light things like balloons have a very low density. You can use the density of objects to predict whether they will sink or float. For instance, things that are less dense than water will float in water. Things that are more dense than water will sink.

Below is a density scale. More dense substances are on the right. Less dense substances are on the left.

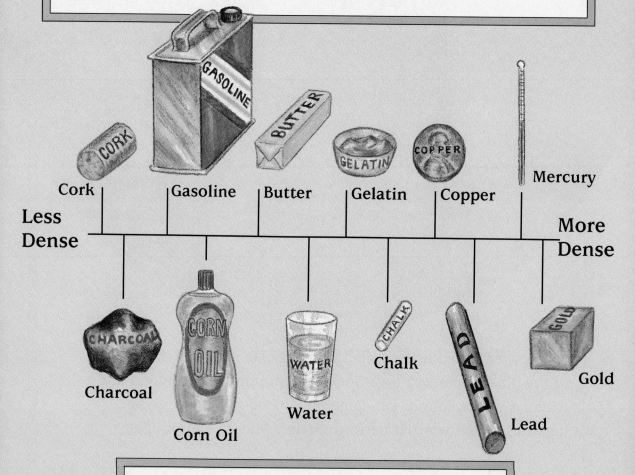

Cork   Gasoline   Butter   Gelatin   Copper   Mercury

Less Dense   **More Dense**

Charcoal   Corn Oil   Water   Chalk   Lead   Gold

Name three things that will float in water.
Name three things that will sink in water.
Name something that will float in Mercury.

THINGS TO THINK ABOUT AND DO

Problem Solving

Imagine that you are a scientist. You discover that the labels are missing from three containers of liquid. How could you find out which liquids have the greatest and least densities?

Show What You Know

1. Why does an egg float in salt water, but sink in tap water?

2. If you know the density of two liquids before you mix them, how can you predict which liquid will sink to the bottom?

3. What is a solution? Give an example.

Creative Writing

Pretend that you are a newspaper reporter. You have been assigned to cover the Talent Show. Write a review of Alvin's magic act. Remember that a review gives the writer's opinion. The review explains what the writer liked and disliked.

ENERGY

Summer in January

by Grace Boyle · illustrated by Susan Gray

"Are you expecting someone?" Maggie's mother asked.

Maggie Clark was looking out the living room window. A thick blanket of snow from a storm the night before covered the neighborhood. The day was sunny and bright, but it was very cold outside.

"Jan said she'd come over today," replied Maggie. "Her aunt gave her a plant for her birthday. It came in a small cardboard box with a plastic window. I told her she could keep it in our greenhouse. Is that okay?"

"Of course," answered Mrs. Clark.

Just then Maggie spotted a bundled figure coming up the front walk to their house. She ran and opened the door.

"Jan!" she cried. "Hurry up! It's getting cold in here!"

Jan couldn't say anything at first because of the scarf wrapped around her face. She took off her mittens and unwrapped her scarf.

"Hi, Maggie. Hello, Mrs. Clark," she finally managed to say.

"Where's your plant?" asked Maggie.

"In here," said Jan, unzipping her jacket and pulling out the box with the plant. "I didn't want it to freeze while I walked over." She handed it to Maggie and took off her boots. "Will your greenhouse be warm enough for my plant, Mrs. Clark?" she asked.

"Oh, yes! In fact, you'll probably want to take off your coat before you go in," she replied.

"Come on," said Maggie. "I'll show you the greenhouse, and then we can go out and build a snow fort."

Maggie and Jan entered the small greenhouse through a door off the kitchen. Immediately they were surrounded by warm air and the pleasant smell of potted plants. The ceiling and walls of the greenhouse were made of glass panels, and the concrete floor was covered by wooden planks. Plants were everywhere. Some hung from beams across the ceiling. Others sat on big tables in the center and along the walls.

"This is great! It's so warm in here," said Jan, taking her plant out of the box and placing it carefully on one of the tables. "It must be 20°C." She walked around the greenhouse looking at the other plants. "What makes the greenhouse so warm?" she asked.

"I don't know," said Maggie. "I guess it's those heaters." She pointed to some heaters along the walls.

Jan went over and put her hand in front of the heaters. "These are hardly even warm. They could never make it 20°C in here. Just look out the window!"

They both looked at the snow piled up outside. They saw a neighbor wearing a down parka shoveling her driveway. Her cheeks were bright red.

"Let's ask my mother how the greenhouse stays warm," Maggie suggested. "After all, she designed it, and she and Dad built it."

They went into the kitchen and asked Mrs. Clark why the greenhouse was so warm. "I don't think you've given it enough thought, girls," she said. "I bet you could figure it out on your own, especially since you like science so much. In fact, I'll give you a challenge. If you can figure out in an hour how the greenhouse is heated and how it stays warm, I'll take you both sledding in Prospect Park."

"Are you serious?" Maggie asked with delight. Prospect Park had the best sledding anywhere.

"Hey, Maggie, let's go!" Jan urged. "There's not a second to waste."

"Now," said Maggie, once they were back in the greenhouse, "where to begin?" She gently touched the leaves of a plant on a sunny table. "This plant is nice and warm. Feel it!"

Jan touched it and nodded. Then she touched a plant in the shade. "This one is much cooler," she said.

"If my cat were in here, she'd be lying on this table," said Maggie, still at the sunny table. "She loves to sleep by the window on sunny days."

"The sun!" they exclaimed at once, and then laughed.

"Of course!" said Jan. "The sun shines through the glass roof and walls of the greenhouse and warms things inside."

"It doesn't warm everything the same, though," said Maggie. "Come over and feel these two pots."

Jan walked over to the sunny table and saw two empty flowerpots sitting side by side. They were both clay, but one was white and the other was dark red. She touched one with each hand.

"That's strange," she said. "The red pot feels warmer than the white one, but they're both in the sun."

"I know why!" Maggie exclaimed. "Dark colors absorb more of the sun's energy than light colors. That makes them feel warm. That's why people wear light-colored clothes in the summer. Light-colored clothes reflect the sun's light. Since the red pot is a darker color, it absorbs more energy."

"That must be another reason why it's so warm in here, then," Jan commented. "Look at all the dark colors: the plants, the tables, the wooden floor, and most of the clay pots. Lots of energy from the sun is being absorbed."

"It's funny," said Maggie, looking out the window. "The wooden floor in here and the deck outside are made of the same wood, but one is warm right now and the other is freezing."

"Yeah. There's ice on the deck," agreed Jan. "But the sun is shining on the deck, just as it is on the wooden floor in here."

"That's true, but the air out there is cold, and the wind is blowing. The deck can't stay warm with the cold wind blowing over it. In here, the wind can't blow the heat away," Maggie responded.

"Right. All this glass must be important, too. Glass lets sunlight in. The plants, pots, and floor absorb the sunlight and warm up. Then the glass traps this heat and keeps most of it inside the greenhouse."

Jan quickly looked at her watch. "We have fifteen minutes to go. Do you think we have it figured out yet?"

"Let's go over what we've discovered," said Maggie. "The glass roof and walls let in sunlight."

"Then the sunlight is absorbed by all the things in the greenhouse, with dark objects absorbing more sunlight than lighter ones," added Jan.

"Right," said Maggie, "and most of the heat is trapped inside the greenhouse by the glass roof and walls."

"And the walls and roof also keep the cold wind from carrying the heat away," said Jan.

"Let's go back early just to show Mom how smart we are!" exclaimed Maggie, and they rushed out of the greenhouse.

As Jan and Maggie entered the kitchen, Mrs. Clark looked up from her work. "Give up already?" she said teasingly. "You still have ten minutes."

"Oh, we figured it out in no time," said Maggie in an off-hand way. "It seemed silly just to wait around."

"All right. So how is a greenhouse heated?" asked her mom.

At a nod from Jan, Maggie gave the explanation just as they had rehearsed it.

"That's absolutely right — and a very good explanation. Congratulations, girls!" Mrs. Clark smiled. Then she looked at Jan and said, "But you still have a question, don't you?"

"Not exactly a question," Jan replied, "but I was thinking of something we learned in school about the greenhouse effect. Our teacher said that Earth's atmosphere lets in sunlight. Then things on Earth's surface absorb the sunlight and warm up. The atmosphere traps much of this heat near the surface. So Earth's atmosphere is like the glass roof of a greenhouse, right?"

"Right, and it's a good thing our atmosphere does trap heat," replied Mrs. Clark. "If all the heat quickly escaped into space, it would get very cold after sunset. But some people are worried. Each year we release more carbon dioxide into the atmosphere by burning fossil fuels such as coal, oil, and natural gas. This extra carbon dioxide could cause the atmosphere to trap more heat. Then Earth's surface temperature would rise."

Mrs. Clark continued, "Scientists don't know how much the temperature might rise. A rise of only a few degrees could affect many plants and animals on Earth. Animals might move to find cooler temperatures. Many plants could die. And think about the polar ice caps! They might begin to melt and cause the level of the oceans to rise."

"Can we do anything to keep this from happening, Mom?" Maggie asked anxiously.

"Well, we can all do our part to help use fossil fuels more efficiently. And we should read what scientists have to say as they learn more about our atmosphere and what affects it. Right now, though, I think we should take some time out to go sledding."

As Maggie and Jan raced to put on their snow gear, Mrs. Clark added, "I think comparing the greenhouse to Earth's atmosphere is worth a bonus. After sledding, we'll stop for lunch."

"Great, Mom! Where?" asked Maggie.

"The Greenhouse Restaurant, where else?" she replied, laughing.

◈ **Reader's Response**
Would you enjoy having a greenhouse? Explain.

The Greenhouse Effect

Some scientists feel the greenhouse effect may be responsible for the warming of the earth's atmosphere. The earth's atmosphere helps trap the sun's heat. The atmosphere allows the sun's light energy to reach the surface of the earth. As sunlight reaches the earth's surface, the light energy is changed to heat energy. Unlike light energy, heat energy cannot easily pass back through the atmosphere into space.

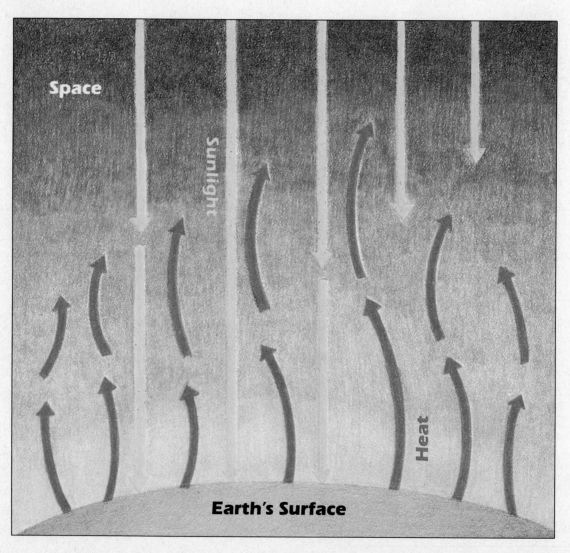

Where does the sun's light energy become heat energy?

Problem Solving

The same light energy from the sun that heats a greenhouse can also heat a home. Think about how you might do this. Draw a diagram to explain your idea. You can use arrows and labels to help explain how it works.

Show What You Know

1. What makes a greenhouse warm? What keeps the heat inside a greenhouse?

2. Compare the glass roof and walls of a greenhouse to Earth's atmosphere. Tell how they are similar.

3. What is the greenhouse effect?

Creative Writing

What if our planet continues to become warmer? Pretend that it is the year 2091, and you are living in the same community you do now. Describe what your community's weather and appearance might be like because of the greenhouse effect.

BERNARDO and the BILLION-YEAR SUNBURN

by Nancy Wood · illustrated by Anne Kennedy

Bernardo was in trouble again. Oscar, his pet lizard, had just scurried past his horrified teacher.

Now Bernardo stood outside the principal's door. "Come in, Bernardo," said Mr. Clark, the principal. "You're a regular visitor."

Bernardo listened politely while Mr. Clark spoke to him about bringing pets to school and disrupting class.

"But Oscar was my favorite lizard," Bernardo explained.

Mr. Clark leaned forward. "Bernardo, this can't continue. This is the third time in six weeks that your teacher has sent you here. You must stay after school for three afternoons next week."

"There goes baseball practice," Bernardo thought with a frown.

Before Mr. Clark dismissed Bernardo, he handed him a piece of paper with five riddles on it.

"A former graduate of our school is an astronaut," Mr. Clark continued. "He just sent me a letter. In it were the five riddles you're holding, two airline tickets to Florida, and two passes to see the next Shuttle launch. The first student to solve all the riddles will be

sent to watch a real Shuttle lift-off with one parent. I'm sending the riddles home with all the students."

"A real rocket launch in Florida?" Bernardo asked, amazed.

"That's right," said Mr. Clark. "Everyone has a chance to win."

Bernardo's face lit up, and Mr. Clark could not help smiling. "When you think you've found an answer to a riddle, write it down, and sign your name. Drop it in that box outside my office. My secretary will log in each entry, record the answers, and tell me when a student has solved all five."

Bernardo looked at the paper and read each clue:

BLUE MARBLE

NIGHT AT NOON

FIERCE WIND WITHOUT AIR

MY FREE-FLOATING CHAIR

FACE WITH A BILLION-YEAR SUNBURN

Good luck, students.

Remember to use all of the resources at your school.

Just nineteen words stood between Bernardo and a chance to see a Shuttle launch. He read them again. Should he find someone with a marble collection or ask a doctor about sunburn? He didn't know where to begin.

"Blue marble . . . blue marble," he said to himself. He had heard those words before. Suddenly, he remembered that it was on a television show. The show began with a picture of Earth from space. Clouds swept across the planet in white wispy streamers. The dark blue ocean, white clouds, and tan continents looked like the swirling colors of a marble.

"That's it! The blue marble is what Earth looks like from space! I already solved the first riddle. Only four more to go!"

After dinner he got out Volume S of the encyclopedia. Under the space entry, he saw pictures of the sun, Earth, and moon. One picture showed a solar eclipse. Bernardo read the words below the picture.

Total Solar Eclipse: When the moon moves directly between Earth and the sun, its shadow falls on part of Earth's surface. Viewers inside this shadow see the dark moon pass in front of the bright sun. If the moon covers the sun's disk completely, the sky becomes dark. Only the sun's faint outer atmosphere, called the corona, can be seen. This darkness can last for up to 7 1/2 minutes.

Bernardo stared at the picture of the solar eclipse. "Darkness in the daytime," he thought. "That's the same thing as 'night at noon.' The answer to the second riddle is a solar eclipse."

The next morning was Saturday. Bernardo had promised to deliver lunch to his sister Ana. She worked at the local college radio station on weekends. Bernardo wanted to show her the riddles, so he brought Volume S along with lunch. Ana was busily turning knobs as he entered the room. She looked annoyed.

"Hey, Ana, what's wrong?" asked Bernardo.

"Just listen to all of this static!" she answered. "I can't get rid of it."

"What makes the static in the first place?" Bernardo asked.

"Right now, the sun is very active with many sunspot regions. Eruptions called flares often occur near these sunspots. Flares produce high energy particles streaming outward from the sun. This stream is called the solar wind. When the strength of the solar wind increases, it can affect Earth's upper atmosphere. Radio broadcasts can become filled with static," his sister explained.

The word "wind" caught Bernardo's attention. "Ana, did you say that the solar wind travels through space between the sun and Earth?" he asked.

Ana nodded her head and began describing how the solar wind interacted with Earth's magnetic field and caused auroras. But Bernardo was no longer listening. He was writing his answer to riddle number three.

Early on Monday, Bernardo dropped his three answers into the box. "What is left?" he thought. "'A free-floating chair' and a 'billion-year sunburn.' Plus the clue about using school resources. I guess it's time to go to the library."

At the library, Bernardo talked to Mrs. Glenn, the librarian. He asked if she had any books or articles about the astronaut who had made up this contest. She pointed to a poster of the astronaut in space. It showed him in a manned maneuvering unit. This rocket-powered backpack with armrest controls lets him float far from the Shuttle. It looked like a chair floating in space.

Bernardo clapped his hand over his mouth. He was afraid he would holler "WOW!" Then the other kids might guess that he had found the answer to the fourth riddle.

"Now to try for the last riddle . . . " he thought. "Maybe the astronaut used the same reference books that are in this library." Bernardo scanned the space-science shelf. He found his clue in a book written before he was born. In a chapter called "The Lunar Surface" he read about conditions unique to the moon. It told of the moon's two-week-long scorching days and its two weeks of freezing night. It also said that solar wind had made permanent changes in the moon's surface over billions of years. The book called this a 'sunburn.'

That was it! Bernardo hurried to turn in the last two answers. He dropped them into the box and hoped he was the first to solve all the riddles correctly.

That evening after supper, Bernardo was sitting on the back steps when he heard the telephone ring. He heard his mom say, "Hello, Mr. Clark." She was quiet for the next minute or two, then she said, "That's fantastic! Bernardo has always wanted to go to a Shuttle launch. Now he'll have that chance." Bernardo could not believe it. He had won!

Looking up at the night sky, Bernardo knew that the moon was still getting its billion-year sunburn. But down here on Earth nothing would ever be the same for him again.

◈ **Reader's Response**

Describe how you would feel if you were Bernardo.

Night at Noon

One of the things Bernardo learned about in the story was a solar eclipse. Below is a diagram of the sun, moon, and the earth during a total solar eclipse. Notice the moon's shadow on the earth.

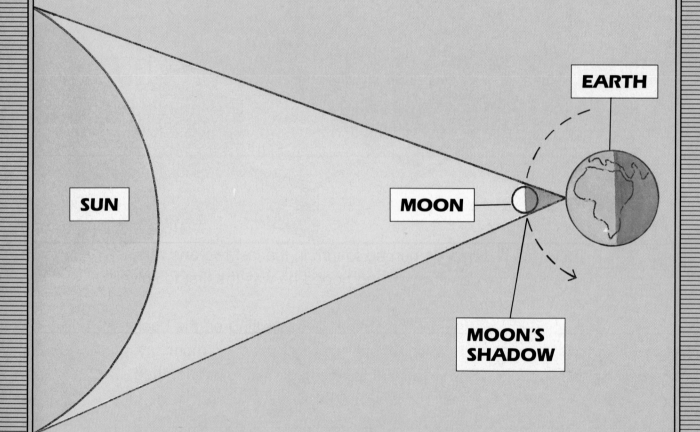

SUN

MOON

EARTH

MOON'S SHADOW

If you witnessed a solar eclipse, what would you see? Suppose you were an astronaut on the moon. What would you see on the earth during this eclipse?

THINGS TO THINK ABOUT AND DO

Problem Solving

Find the answers to each of the riddles below. Use Bernardo's answers in the story to help solve these riddles.

Man-made Answer

Seen from Earth

It's Been A Long Day

Show What You Know

1. Why is Earth called a "blue marble?"
2. Describe how a solar eclipse occurs.
3. What do the billion-year sunburn and static have in common?

Creative Writing

Create three riddles like the ones that Bernardo solved. The answer to your riddles should be about the sun, moon, or one of the planets. See if your classmates can solve your space riddles.

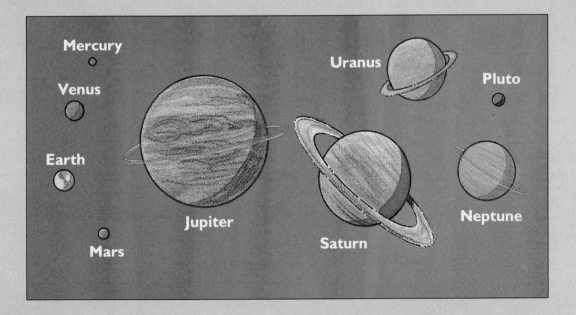

EARTH

RIVERS OF GOLD

by Kathlyn Gay · illustrated by John Holder

Pushing open the tent flap, Jed Shelby shivered in the cool
night air of the Colorado hills. Through pine branches he could see
the first stars appearing. He thought of his mother and younger
brother and sister far away in Missouri.

Jed and his father had left home for Colorado months ago, soon
after his father had gotten a letter from Jed's Uncle Pete. Jed could
still remember every word of Uncle Pete's letter.

December 2, 1859

Dear Bill,

I have been prospecting in California
with two friends of mine. We hear there
is plenty of gold in Colorado and plan
to go there in the spring. Why don't
you join us? Prospecting is a pretty
rough life. You'd better come alone.
As soon as we stake a claim and
find some gold you can have your
family come out to Colorado, too.

Your brother,
Pete

Jed remembered the night the letter came. He could hear his parents talking softly, and he knew they were discussing whether or not his father should go to Colorado. When Jed got up the next morning, he saw his father staring out the window. Jed knew then that his father had decided to meet Uncle Pete in Colorado.

Jed begged his father to take him along. He promised to work twice as hard as anyone else and to never complain. At first his father said no, but Jed pleaded and, finally, his father agreed. The trip to Colorado had taken longer than Jed had expected.

As he thought about his family back in Missouri, Jed felt a strange tightness in his throat. He hated to admit he was homesick. He had been so proud to be allowed to come. But the life of a prospector was hard for a ten-year old.

All that day Jed, his father, Uncle Pete, and his uncle's two friends had trudged through bushes and climbed over big rocks, following a narrow, fast-flowing river. At sunset they had set up camp along a bank lined with huge boulders.

In the tent now his father slept, rolled tightly in a blanket. He was snoring loudly. Jed couldn't close his eyes. He was too excited.

Tomorrow they planned to pan along the river. Uncle Pete figured they had a good chance of finding gold. Uncle Pete had learned about prospecting in California.

"Looks like we'll find some 'placer gold,'" he'd declared.

"What do you mean by that?" Jed had asked.

"Well," Uncle Pete explained, "placer gold is gold that is mixed in with sand and gravel. If there is any placer gold in this river, it is washed out of the granite mountains by streams and rivers.

"Placer gold is also known as 'poor man's deposits,'" Uncle Pete continued, "because the gold is close to the surface. That makes it cheap to mine. If we're lucky, some flakes and pieces of placer gold will have washed up to the gravel near the river bottom here." Uncle Pete pointed to the boulders along the shore of the river. "We might find pieces of placer gold caught between those rocks."

Jed curled up in his blanket and finally dropped off to sleep. He awoke to find that the men had already gone down to the river to pan for gold. Jed pulled on his boots, stuffed two biscuits in his pocket, and grabbed a tin pan.

Jed decided not to join the men right away. He would try panning on his own.

Jed ate his biscuits as he walked to the shallow river. He took the tin pan and waded in. He squatted and scooped some sand and water into his pan. Holding the pan under the water, he swirled the mixture to let the fine sand float out over the edge. He had learned that gold is about eight times more dense than sand, and that the dense particles of gold always settle to the bottom. He hoped to find gold at the bottom of his pan.

Jed scooped and swirled until the cold water made his arms and hands feel numb. He could no longer hear the men's voices clearly. Looking up, he realized he had moved quite a distance from the camp. He'd try one more scoop and —

"WAHOO! What do you know?" Jed whistled through his teeth as he plucked a shiny yellow rock from the pan. He hopped out of the water and raced along the bank, the glistening, glittering stone clutched tightly in his hand.

As he ran toward his father and the other men, Jed couldn't hold in his excitement any longer. "Gold! Gold! I've found gold!" he shouted.

"Calm down, boy, or you'll bring every prospector in the Pacific Northwest down here," Uncle Pete grumbled. "Let's see what you've got."

Jed handed the rock to his uncle. It caught the sun's rays and sparkled as Uncle Pete turned it over in his hand. The other men crowded around as Jed's uncle carefully inspected the material.

Uncle Pete didn't say a word. Instead, he went over to the smoldering campfire and stirred the embers with his shovel. He threw some dry twigs on the fire and they started to burn immediately. Then he dropped Jed's rock into a pan and placed it over the fire.

Jed opened his mouth but couldn't speak.

"What do you think you're doing?" Jed's father stepped in, grabbing his brother by the arm.

"This stuff looks like fools' gold, or pyrite, which is just iron and sulfur," Uncle Pete explained. "If it's real gold, the heat won't hurt it. But pyrite will smoke and, pretty soon . . . "

"It smells terrible!" Jed held his nose. He watched as Uncle Pete dumped the pyrite on a rock and hit it with a hammer. It shattered into many pieces.

"Gold wouldn't break like this," Uncle Pete said. "It would just flatten out."

Uncle Pete tousled Jed's hair and laughed. Then he buried the pyrite in the ground and walked back to the river bank with the other men.

Jed followed. "What's going on?" he asked his father.

His father pointed to a long wooden box sitting at the river's edge. The box looked like an oversized cradle. An iron plate pierced with holes covered its top. "We built two of these cradles early this morning. I'm surprised you didn't hear us pounding. Come on and help me. It works best with two people."

Jed's father shoveled sand and gravel onto the iron plate. He told Jed to pour buckets of water over the mixture while he rocked the box.

"These will catch any gold in the mixture," Jed's father said, pointing to the narrow strips of wood nailed to the floor of the box.

Jed's eyes, searching for gold, fastened on his father's narrow wedding band. "You already have some gold, Dad," he said, pointing to the ring.

"That's right, Jed." Dad smiled. "Of course it's not pure gold. It's an alloy."

"What's an alloy?" asked Jed.

"An alloy is a mixture of two or more metals. For example, gold is usually mixed with silver, copper, and other metals," his father explained. "This hardens the gold and makes it wear better. Now let's get back to work. Keep pouring the water while I dump in some more sand and gravel."

As the water and sand swished through the box, some of the more dense materials settled along the wooden strips nailed to the bottom.

Jed wrinkled his nose. "It doesn't look like anything to me."

"Be patient," his father said. "We just got started."

For over an hour, Jed and his father worked the cradle while small mounds of washed sand piled up along the river bank. Not once did they see even the tiniest glimmer in the dark box.

"Maybe this isn't a good place to find gold after all," Jed sighed. But as soon as he had spoken, he grabbed the cradle.

"Shake it, Dad!" he yelled. "I saw something. There! Look!" Jed almost fell into the cradle as he watched his father carefully take out a stone about the size of a pea. It was covered with sand, but Jed could see the luster underneath.

Jed tried to hold back his excitement. "How do we know it's gold and not pyrite?"

"It's gold," his father whispered. He took the nugget over to a rock and tapped it with his hammer. The nugget began to flatten out.

"See?" he said. "Pyrite would have shattered. This river could be full of gold. Let's go and show the others what we found."

Jed skipped along the bank behind his father. He was grinning so broadly that his face hurt. Jed was dreaming of the day when his whole family would be together again.

◈ **Reader's Response**

How would you feel if you were far away from your home and family?

MINERAL PROPERTIES

Minerals are natural substances found in Earth's crust. Jed and other prospectors identified gold and other minerals by their physical properties. A physical property is anything that we can observe or measure. These pictures illustrate some of the properties of minerals.

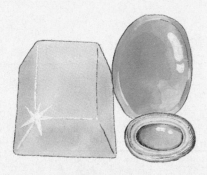

Luster

Density

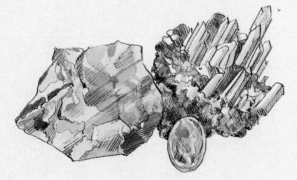

Color

Hardness

How did Jed use some of these properties to identify gold?

How do these properties affect how gold is used?

PROBLEM SOLVING

You are taking a hike in the woods and you find a shiny rock. You think it might be a diamond. What steps can you take to find out if it really is a diamond?

SHOW WHAT YOU KNOW

1. How can you tell the difference between pyrite and gold?
2. Why was the cradle an effective tool for gold prospectors?
3. What is an alloy?

CREATIVE WRITING

Pretend you are Jed. Write a letter home to your family in Missouri telling them about your experiences prospecting for gold in Colorado.

DOUBLE

by James W. Manley • illustrated by Marcus Hamilton

"It's really happening!" Hiroshi said, his eyes shining with excitement. "We're going to Alaska for the summer!"

"I know. I can hardly believe it!" his sister Yasuko sighed happily.

Spread out on the table before them were maps and pictures. Next to Yasuko was a growing list of campsites and interesting places to visit along the way. As Yasuko was adding "Jed's Tower of Hubcaps" to the list, she heard her father come up behind her.

"This is going to be a fantastic trip!" Yasuko exclaimed. "We've decided to keep a journal as we travel."

"A journal," Hiroshi explained, "is a book in which you write down data. We'll take turns writing in it."

"What kinds of things will you write?" their dad asked.

"Hmm..," said Yasuko, thinking for a moment. They hadn't

RAINBOWS

quite worked out that part. "I think we should write down all the 'firsts,'" she decided.

"What's a *first*?" asked Hiroshi and Dad.

"You know," Yasuko replied, "anything we see for the first time or do for the first time. Stuff like that."

"That's cool." Hiroshi nodded. "But we won't be seeing firsts all the time. We need other things to record."

"How about recording temperature and air-pressure readings all along the trip," their dad suggested.

"But how do we measure air pressure?" asked Hiroshi.

"We can bring Grandpa's old barometer along. Its air-pressure readings will tell us when the weather is going to change," said Dad.

For once, Hiroshi and Yasuko were in perfect agreement.

They left Ohio on the Fourth of July in a thunder and lightning storm. "It's like having our own personal fireworks to begin our trip," said Hiroshi.

"That's a first!" Yasuko exclaimed as she started to write down what Hiroshi just said.

"What?" asked an embarrassed Hiroshi. "What did I do that was a first?"

"You said the first interesting thing on the trip," Yasuko replied with a smile.

The list of firsts grew daily, as did the weather readings. Keeping track of the data was fun for a while, but as they drove through the flat plains of the Midwest, the air pressure didn't change much.

Each day Yasuko recorded temperature and Hiroshi recorded air pressure anyway. As they started climbing the foothills of the Rocky Mountains, Yasuko made a disturbing discovery.

"You broke Grandpa's barometer, Hiroshi," she said.

"No, I didn't," he replied. "And why do you think it's broken anyway?"

"The weather hasn't changed in three days, but the barometer is showing lower numbers. Look at the journal. Yesterday the barometer averaged above 30 inches. Today the readings are below 30. It's got to be broken," explained Yasuko.

"Hold on, kids," said their dad. "Look at your data and think about where we are. Is there anything that has changed besides the barometer readings?"

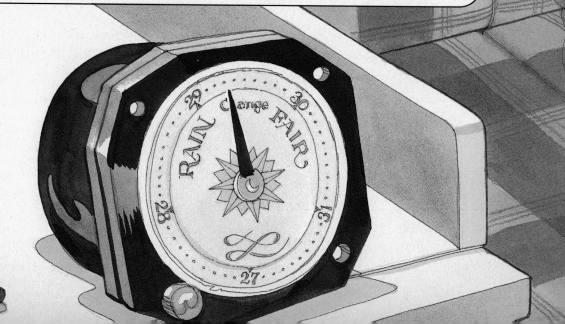

"The temperature readings follow the same pattern every day," Yasuko answered.

"But the scenery is changing," added Hiroshi. "There are mountains around and in front of us. Does the air pressure have something to do with where we are?"

"Sure it does," Yasuko exclaimed. "Air pressure is caused by the weight of the air over us. If we climb up a mountain, there is less air above us and the air pressure must drop. Right, Dad?"

"That's it, Yasuko. Two things affect the air pressure. The height of the air column over your head, and the weight of the air column."

"Is some air heavier than other air?" asked Hiroshi.

"Yes," said Dad. "Cold dry air is heavier than warm moist air. Look at your barometer readings, Hiroshi. Do they change slightly each night?"

Hiroshi looked at the journal. "You're right, Dad. Each morning the barometric pressure is a little higher than it was the evening before."

Yasuko peered over his shoulder. "That makes sense. The morning air is cooler and heavier. So the air pressure rises during the night."

Yasuko and Hiroshi decided to pay closer attention to the temperature and how it compared with the air pressure. They also decided to record elevation information as they traveled. They found signs by the highway, at bridges, and at airports. Tourist stops and post offices also gave information. What they didn't look for were changes in the sky.

"Something's wrong," announced Hiroshi. "The land has been flat for miles and the temperature hasn't changed, but the barometer keeps falling." No one noticed that the sky to the southwest was growing darker.

The wind picked up as they prepared dinner at their campsite. Hiroshi checked the barometer again. "The reading has dropped in just the short time we've been camped," he said.

Yasuko looked up. "Maybe the air is changing," she replied.

Meanwhile the sky darkened even more. A gigantic, gray, umbrella-shaped cloud moved across the sky from the southwest. The wind grew stronger.

"Forget dinner!" Dad yelled from the camper. "Everyone come inside!"

As they scrambled into the camper, they heard a radio announcer report that a tornado watch was in effect.

"Open the windows part way," Dad ordered. "Watch for a funnel-shaped cloud." He pointed to a deep ditch near the camper. "If the tornado comes, we'll get into the ditch. Remember to cover the back of your head and neck with your arms and hands. Stay down until the tornado passes."

The heavy camper rocked from side to side as the wind and rain pounded on it. "The barometer dropped to 29.7," said Hiroshi, "but it seems to be rising now."

"That's normal for a storm like this," Dad explained.

They waited and watched the storm. Yasuko wrote in the journal about their first tornado watch. Dad hunted through the static on the radio for the local news.

An hour passed. The barometer continued to climb slowly and the sky began to clear. Eventually the radio broadcasted news that the tornado watch had been lifted.

Hiroshi, Yasuko, and their father went out of the camper and looked around. It was then that they noticed another first.

"A double rainbow," Yasuko whispered, gazing at the sky.

"Where did the second rainbow come from?" asked Hiroshi.

"When sunlight passes through water droplets in the sky, the light separates into colors and makes a rainbow," answered Dad. "Actually, two rainbows are always made, but it's usually not possible to see the second one. Notice that the second rainbow is much fainter than the first and that the colors appear in the reverse order. If the sky were light, it would be hard to see the second rainbow. But since the sky is still dark from the storm, we can see both rainbows."

"So double rainbows are happy endings to bad storms," said Yasuko. Dad smiled and agreed, and Hiroshi quickly added that thought to the journal.

Later he said to his sister, "To think we thought weather was boring! This has been a great trip, and we haven't even reached Alaska yet."

◈ Reader's Response

If you were to keep a journal while on a trip, what kinds of things would you write about?

Tornado Facts and Safety Rules

A tornado is a small funnel of rapidly spinning air. The air pressure in the center of the funnel is very low, so winds rush toward it. Wherever the funnel touches the ground, it acts like a gigantic vacuum cleaner. Objects as large as trucks and mobile homes are pushed into the funnel by high winds. These winds can reach speeds as high as 800 kilometers per hour.

More tornadoes occur in the United States than in any other part of the world. They often occur during heavy thunderstorms and can travel very fast — up to 116 kilometers per hour. Therefore, there is often very little warning before a tornado strikes.

If you do hear about a tornado warning, you should follow these safety rules:

If you are inside: go to a storm cellar, basement, or first floor room with no windows. Lie flat under a heavy piece of furniture if you are in a first floor room. Never stand near a window. Never go to an attic.

If you are outdoors: lie face-down in a low place, like a ditch, and cover your head with your hands.

What causes the high wind speeds in a tornado?

PROBLEM SOLVING

Hiroshi and Yasuko's father knew that a storm was headed their way. How could you predict a weather change in your area? What signs would you look for?

SHOW WHAT YOU KNOW

1. What does a barometer measure?
2. What happens to a barometer during a big storm?
3. What makes a rainbow?

CREATIVE WRITING

If Yasuko and Hiroshi knew how to use the barometer readings to forecast weather, they would not have been surprised by the storm. Write about a time a change in weather surprised you or changed your plans. Was there a way for you to have predicted the weather on that occasion?

The Amazing
BODY MAZE

by Kathy W. Peiffer • illustrated by Scott Pollack

"It's time to play THE AMAZING BODY — the game that takes you to some fantastic places. Now audience, let's meet today's contestants. Please give a big round of applause to Dennis Gardner and Tawny Mendez."

Dennis and Tawny ran out on stage. They were dressed in white bodysuits covered with large round stickers. Some of the stickers said *Nitrogen*, *Oxygen* and *Carbon dioxide*. Others read *Dust* or *Pollen*.

"What are you?" the grinning emcee asked.

"We're air," Dennis replied.

"And what are these stickers all over your suits?" the emcee asked Tawny.

"They're some of the different things you find in the air, like nitrogen, oxygen, and carbon dioxide. And dust and pollen, too."

"Okay! Now, kids, since you're air, which systems in The Amazing Body Maze are you going to travel through?"

"The respiratory and circulatory systems!" they replied.

"Right again! Okay, contestants! Each of you will enter The Amazing Body Maze through the respiratory system," he said, pointing to the huge clear plastic model of the human body. "The first person to reach today's target, exchange three oxygen stickers for carbon dioxide stickers, and return through the lungs is our winner.

The wheel labels read: Bladder, Liver, Big Toe, Thumb, Appendix, Pancreas, Brain, Stomach, Kidneys, Knee cap, Ear, Hip

"And remember, contestants," the emcee continued, "almost anything can happen along the way. So let's not waste another minute. It's time to spin our Amazing Body Dial to see where you're going."

A smiling assistant walked over to a large wheel of chance and gave it a turn. As it clicked past a dozen possible targets, members of the audience shouted, "Go to the brain! Go to the pancreas! The appendix!" The dial slowly ticked to a halt on the spot labeled "Big Toe."

"Okay, contestants, that's where you must go. Now Gary, tell Dennis and Tawny what the person who gets through first will win."

The announcer's booming voice filled the sound stage. "Today, one lucky person will win a hot-air balloon ride over the Rocky Mountains, plus a complete set of the *Encyclopedia Humongous*."

"Don't forget," the emcee resumed, "the first one to reach a big toe, exchange oxygen stickers for carbon dioxide stickers, and return to us is our winner. Tawny, Dennis, are you ready?"

Dennis and Tawny nodded.

"Go!" shouted the emcee.

In a flash Dennis ran into the Amazing Body Maze through the mouth. Tawny climbed in through the nose. The audience could see them move through the clear plastic.

At the back of the mouth, Dennis faced two passageways from which to choose. One was the esophagus, part of the digestive system, and the other was the trachea, or windpipe. Dennis knew he wanted the windpipe, but which was which? He could hear the audience yelling advice.

As he stood there trying to decide, a rush of water knocked him off his feet. The Amazing Body Maze was taking a drink! Dennis was washed down the esophagus.

Dennis was entering the digestive system! He grabbed on to the gate that guards the stomach. Just as he was thinking that he had no chance of winning, The Amazing Body Maze burped and pushed him back up into the mouth.

Tawny was having better luck. She ran through the narrow nasal passage where hundreds of small hairs, called cilia, caught and tore off two of her dust and pollen stickers.

Then suddenly, something went terribly wrong. The walls of the nose began shaking. The hairs tickled her. Then, with a gigantic rush of air and a loud KACHOO, she found herself back outside the maze. She had been thrown out of the Body Maze by a sneeze!

"Too bad, Tawny," the emcee cried. "The pollen and dust got stuck on the hairs and caused a sneeze."

"So that's what it was!" She quickly removed her remaining pollen and dust stickers. Then she saw Dennis pop out of the mouth.

"I'm not taking another chance going in that way," he announced. He saw Tawny peeling off her pollen and dust stickers and did the same.

The race was back on. Tawny and Dennis both entered the nose. Free of dust and pollen, they easily ran through the nasal passages, past the back of the mouth, and down the windpipe. When they came to the place where the windpipe divided, they both entered the lungs through a bronchial tube. They slid down smaller and smaller tubes until they landed inside the alveoli, air sacs that looked like clusters of balloons.

"The air sacs!" Tawny exclaimed.

"That's right, audience," the emcee was saying. "Now Tawny and Dennis are just one cell away from leaving the respiratory system and entering the circulatory system."

Tawny knew that she should be able to break through the thin wall that separated the air sac from the capillary. But for some reason she couldn't push through.

"There's got to be an entrance here somewhere," Dennis said.

"I've got it!" Tawny said excitedly. "The blood in the capillaries will take oxygen at this point, but not carbon dioxide." She ripped off all her carbon dioxide stickers, leaving just the oxygen and nitrogen. Then she was able to push easily through the thin wall of the air sac into the capillary.

Dennis didn't believe her until she disappeared through the wall. Then he quickly peeled off his carbon dioxide stickers.

"This girl knows her stuff," the emcee declared. The audience shouted its approval.

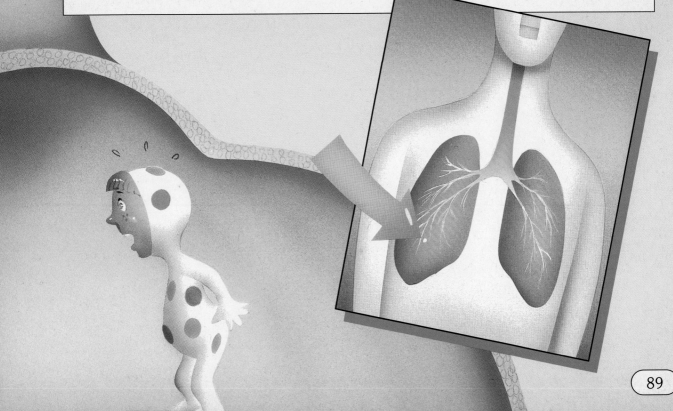

89

When Tawny came out on the other side of the wall, she was amazed to find a busy river filled with little red, white, and clear plastic boats. The boats were blood cells. Knowing that only red blood cells carry oxygen, Tawny jumped into a red boat and grabbed the steering wheel.

Dennis followed in hot pursuit. He jumped into another red boat and raced after Tawny.

"Now we've got a race," the emcee shouted. Half the crowd screamed "Go Tawny" and the other half chanted "DEN-NIS, DEN-NIS, DEN-NIS."

Tawny didn't notice the noise from the audience. Her attention was on a rhythmic thumping sound inside the maze. As it grew louder, she knew she was heading straight for the heart. She clutched the steering wheel as the forward flow of the river swept her through the heart and into a large artery.

At a fork in the river, Tawny made a quick decision and spun her wheel to the left. She now was in the left leg artery, speeding toward the left big toe. She turned to look for Dennis. He was not in sight! Her heart rose — until she faced front again. Ahead a group of white blood cells was fighting. She could not steer around the cells, and she found herself

being swept helplessly into the battle.

"Oh-oh, folks," said the emcee. "Tawny has encountered a jam-up: white blood cells fighting bacteria. She's going to lose valuable time!"

Dennis was having no such problems. When he saw Tawny turn down the artery to the left leg, he had decided to see if he could make up time by going down the right leg. In no time Dennis arrived in the right big toe.

Immediately he tore off his oxygen stickers, pushed them through the thin capillary wall, and pulled carbon dioxide stickers from one of the cells. Now all he had to do was steer through the veins until he reached the heart and lungs. He gave a victory wave and the audience went wild.

"It's not over yet," the emcee cautioned the audience. "Remember, folks: in the Amazing Body Maze, anything can happen."

After bumping back and forth a lot, Tawny finally managed to pass the jam of white blood cells and complete her journey to the left big toe. She exchanged her oxygen for carbon dioxide, and then steered into a small vein for the return trip to the heart and lungs.

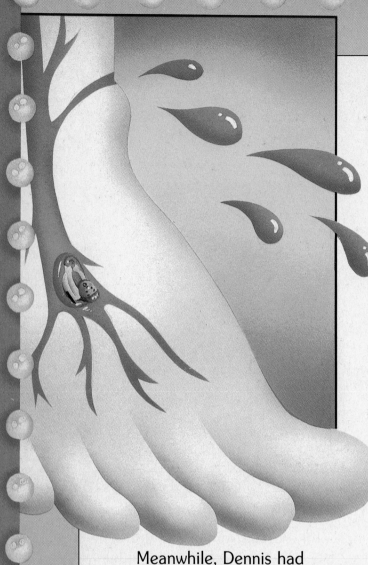

Body Maze — by a completely different route.

Drifting along at a leisurely pace, Dennis suddenly felt a strong pull to the right. No matter how hard he steered to the left, the little red blood-cell boat still pulled to the right. He sat helplessly as his cell, along with other red, white, and clear cells, streamed out of the maze at an opening just above the ankle.

"What happened?" Dennis shouted at the emcee. "There shouldn't be an opening here."

"It's a cut. We told you that anything could happen," the emcee announced.

The race was over, and Dennis knew it. There was no chance he could win now, not unless Tawny also exited through a cut. But that didn't seem likely.

Now all the spectators cheered Tawny on. She guided her boat through the system of larger and larger veins back through the heart to the lungs. Firmly clutching her carbon dioxide stickers, she left her red blood-cell boat, passed through an air sac, and traveled back up through the bronchial tubes. Soon she was out of the lungs, through the windpipe, and out the mouth.

Meanwhile, Dennis had relaxed completely. He knew the pumping action of the heart would pull him back to the lungs without his having to work very hard. He also knew that one-way valves in the leg vein would keep him from slipping back. Once he reached the lungs, the diaphragm would force air out of the lungs and into the windpipe. This would push him out through the nose or mouth. What Dennis did not know was that he would soon exit the Amazing

The audience was cheering! Dennis smiled and shook her hand. "Congratulations. That maze was tough!"

"We have our winner, folks," the emcee announced. "You know, Tawny, we give all our winners the opportunity to come back and play again. How about it? Do you want to take the prizes you've won today and go home? Or will you come back tomorrow and play again — this time in the digestive system as a food particle?"

The audience screamed, "YES! SAY YES! COME BACK!"

Tawny looked at the Maze. "No, thank you!" she laughed. "I'll read about the digestive system in my new encyclopedia, instead. One trip through the Amazing Body Maze is enough for anyone!"

◈ Reader's Response

If you were Tawny, would you want to play "The Amazing Body" again? Why or why not?

Tomorrow **The Digestive System**

The Respiratory System

This diagram of the human body shows the respiratory system.

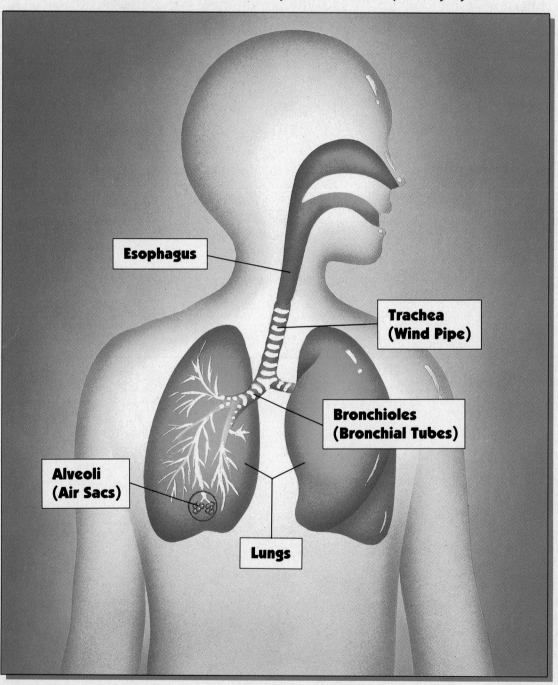

On the diagram, trace the path that air follows through the respiratory system.

Problem Solving

Suppose you were blindfolded and taken to the heart of The Amazing Body Maze. How would you determine where you were? Describe the route you would take to make your escape.

Show What You Know

1. Describe the function of the parts of the respiratory system.

2. Describe the route that air takes through the respiratory system.

3. How does the circulatory system help get oxygen to cells in the body?

Creative Writing

Pretend that you are Tawny or Dennis and are writing about The Amazing Body Maze in your diary. Describe your experiences and explain how you felt at the time. How did you feel at the end, when you realized you'd won or lost?

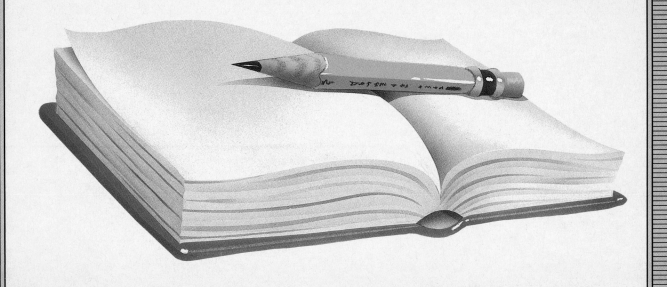